THE LITTLE FILIPINO
ISDAMAN

STORY
PAUL BACERA

ILLUSTRATION
MARK BACERA

ROUNDED SPECS PUBLISHING LLC
ISBN 978-1-952343-05-6

Come on down to the land of the Philippines,
To a land full of palm trees and luscious greens.

Isdaman's on the job, and he will never fail—
He swims fast like a shark, and is strong like a whale.

(And last is a trick that he hides up his sleeves—
He can turn into a fish anytime he believes!)

"Oh, please, you're so weak—I will break all your bones. Just one look in my eyes and you'll turn into stone!"

As the Snake Lady raged, our brave Isdaman fought.
Every strike cleanly dodged, every punch firmly caught.

His quick skill and his plan, they had worked like a charm.
Her fangs missed the fish and she bit her own arm!

With great shock, she passed out without further a wail.
Our brave hero changed back and threw her into jail.

To the jungle he went, needing no rest or break,
To find out who had sent the malevolent snake.

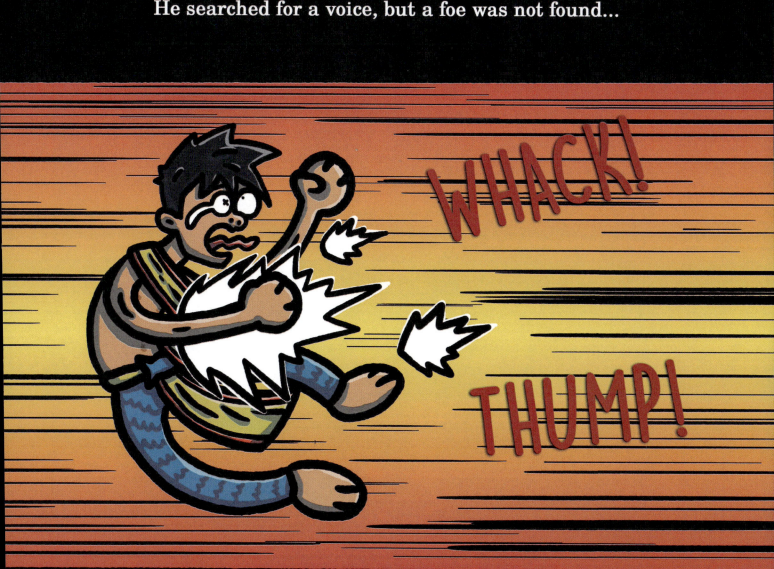

And again the voice roared, "Oh, you don't have a clue! I'm completely invisible—what will you do?"

A **WHAM** and a **BAM!** Punches struck head and chest.
And a **BAM** and a **WHAM!** Fists flew in, right and left.

A man then appeared, coming out from thin air.
He grinned, then he laughed, "Ha! You thought I'd fight fair?!"

Our hero, he fought, though it seemed like a slaughter.
He got hit and he soared, plunging into the water.

"I won't run, I won't hide. I'll do all that I can!
I'll push through, that's my word, 'cause I am Isdaman!"

An idea popped up. With a **POOF** he swam faster.
And the waves grew in size, with that fish as the master.

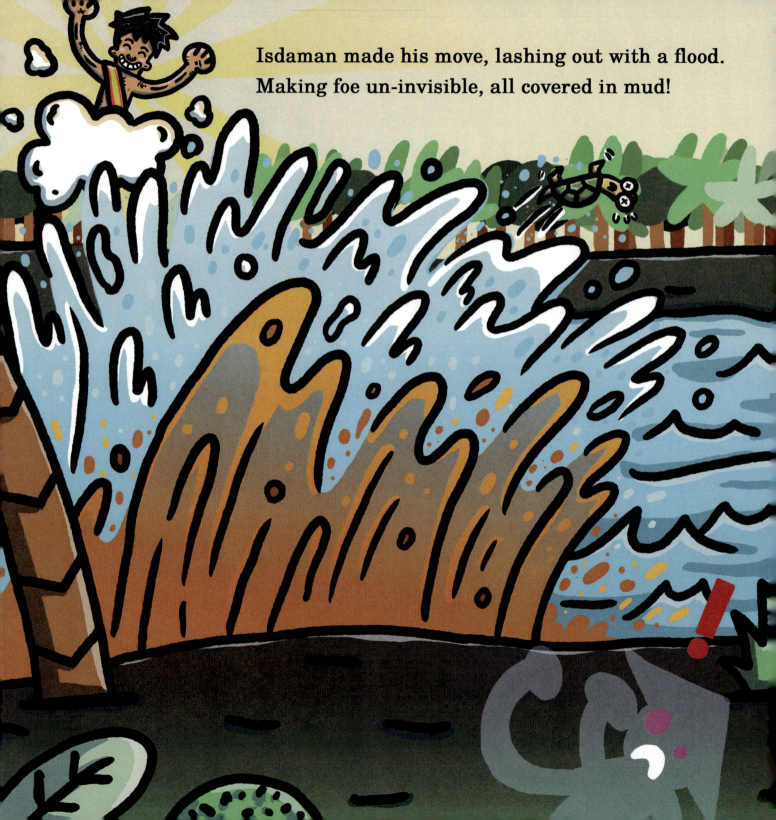

(In the trees of the jungle, *kapre* live and tarry.
Giant, muscular beasts that are big, dark, and hairy.)

Isdaman couldn't wait, rushing in for the brute.
But Dupree grabbed a tree, yanked it out by its roots.

And he charged once again, aimed towards the *kapre*.
But this time, from behind, where Dupree couldn't see.

Then a **SMACK!** Like *lamok*,
Our poor hero was swatted.
But he rose up again,
Full of thought as he plotted.

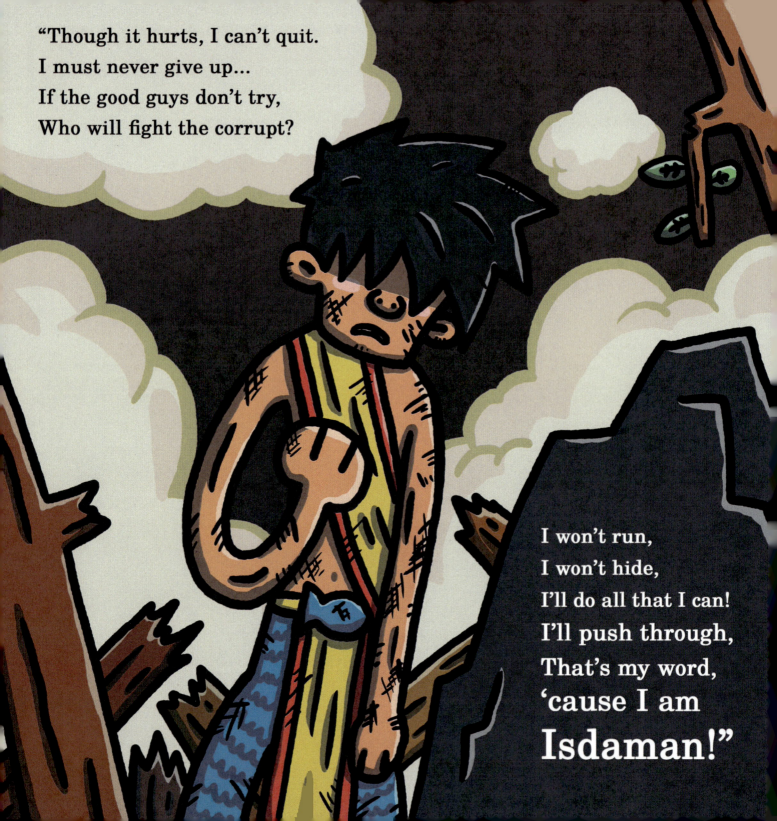

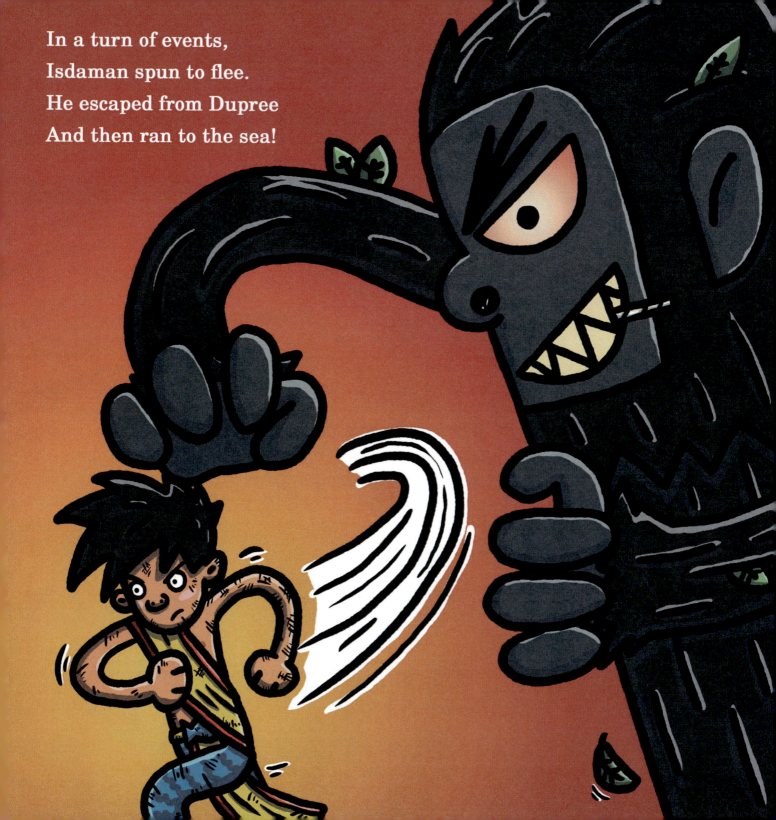

"Hey, *duwag*, come on back! Don't you dare think we're done."
Wicked grin touched his eyes, "It was just getting fun!"

The big beast bounded up, then he chased even faster.
Isdaman changed his shape and leapt into the water.

But Dupree soon found out,
In the course of his badgering.
Tens of thousands of fish
All around him were gathering.

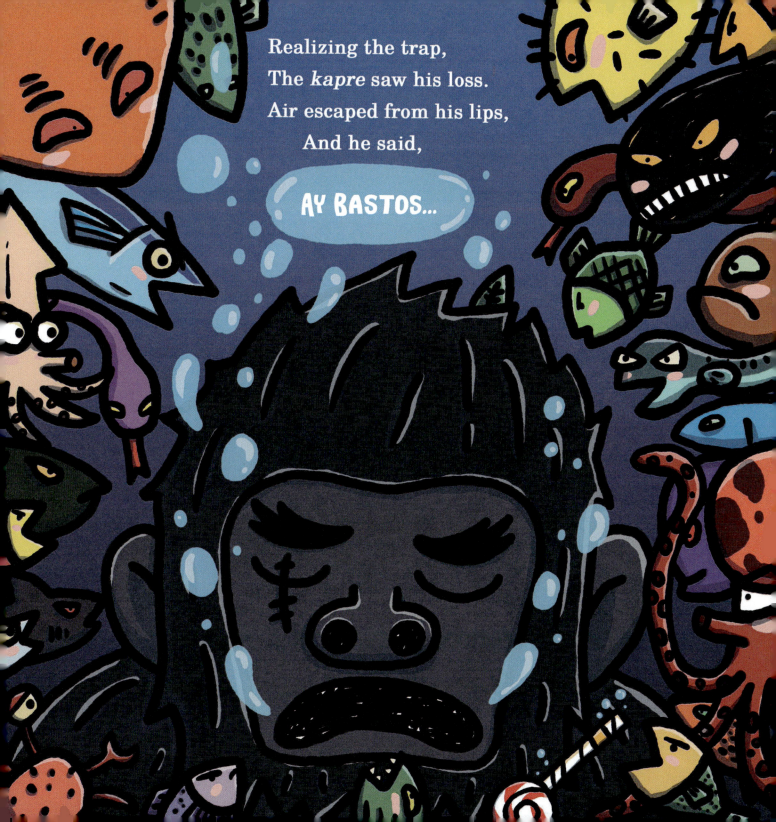

Isdaman gave a cue—thousands swam at Dupree.
The fish bound him and left him, abandoned at sea.

The *kapre* was now exiled. The battle was done.
Whether snake, man, or beast—our *bayani* had won!

For the *kampeon*, the town threw a big celebration.
All the families were safe, they had found liberation.

From this point, his fame spread far, and all through the land,
As the hero that said, "I'll do all that I can!"

So don't ever give up. Just believe that you can!
Even *you* can push through, because

YOU IS THE MAN!

About the Chocolate Hills

The Chocolate Hills are a spread of dome-shaped hills located in the center of the island province of Bohol in the Central Visayas region of the Philippines.

Legend has it that in ancient times, two giants had a fight and threw rocks and boulders at each other. The result of their quarrel was the formation of giant hills.

Science has revealed that erosion and rainfall combined to form these 1,776 magnificent mounds known today as the Chocolate Hills for their resemblance to a popular teardrop-shaped chocolate candy. They are one of the most beautiful natural formations in the world and were declared as a National Geological Monument.

WORDS TO KNOW

The following Filipino words are scattered throughout the story. These are their English counterparts.

Isda - Fish
Bangus - Milkfish
Pasensya - I'm sorry
Ngayon - Now
Kapre - Folklore giant
Lamok - Mosquito
Duwag - Coward
Ay Bastos - How rude!
Higante - Giant
Bayani - Hero
Kampeon - Champion

About the Author & Illustrator

Paul Bacera

Paul Bacera is a filmmaker and Youtube creator. Being raised Filipino, he has always had a love for Asian culture, history, and entertainment. His channel, The Asian Theory, is a celebration of all those values.
Visit it at www.youtube.com/c/theasiantheory

Mark Bacera

Mark Bacera is a bestselling children's book author and illustrator most known for his Bewildering Body series. The said series includes his first picture book, The Poo Poo Book, published in 2018. The author lives in western Japan with his wonderful wife & daughter who also participate in the creative process and making of other books. To see more of his works, visit:
www.amazon.com/mark-bacera/e/B0198EHT0M
Or email him at: mark@roundedspecspublishing.com

Authors love reviews! To leave one, visit:
https://amzn.to/2OtcvqH

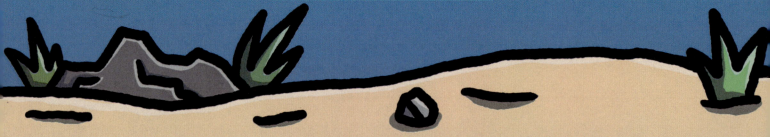

Other Books by Rounded Specs

- The Poo Poo Book
- The Belly Button Book
- The Fart Book
- The Booger Book
- The Snot Book
- The Tooth Book
- The Stinky Feet Book
- The Ear Wax Book
- The Sweat Book
- The Tear Book
- The Spit Book
- Baby Poop
- A Naughty Kid's Christmas ABC Story
- I'm an Alien-Vampire and I'm Proud of It!
- A Day With Mae
- Ame the Cat
- Ame Goes to Japan

Please note that some of the above titles have yet to be published. To support us and be notified when new books are in the works and released, send us an email at
<u>info@roundedspecspublishing.com</u>

Made in the USA
Las Vegas, NV
30 April 2023